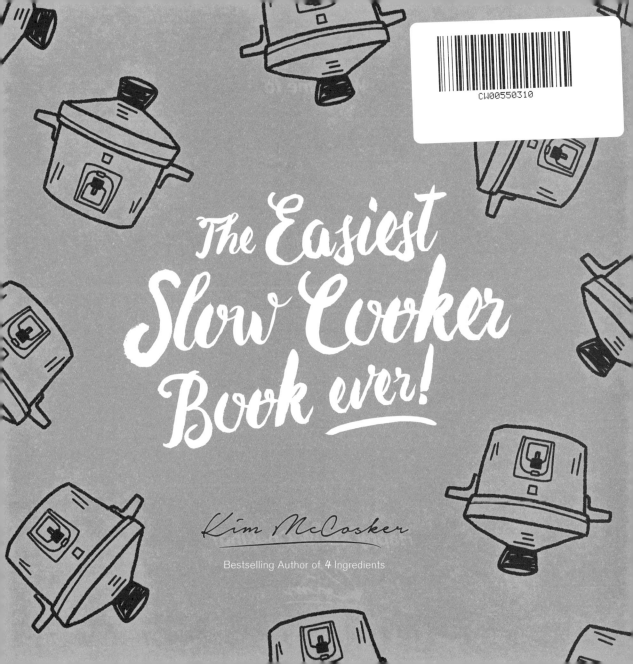

# The Easiest Slow Cooker Book ever!

### Kim McCosker

Bestselling Author of 4 Ingredients

**Welcome to**

# The Easiest Slow Cooker Book ever!

With about **4** million things to squeeze into a day,
I find my slow cooker helps... *ENORMOUSLY!*

I've been using mine for years.
*I'M LITERALLY IN LOVE WITH IT!*

Using a slow cooker is easy, versatile and economical.
It's also a huge time saver, is a brilliant veggie-smuggler and provides
sheer relief and joy when, at the end of a busy day, you walk into
your home with an amazing aroma and the knowledge that dinner is done.

To top it all off, the food that comes from a slow cooker is just delicious.
My slow cooker is one of my best friends and I hope through the ease of
the recipes in this book that it becomes yours too.

**Happy SLOW Cooking!**

*Kim*

# PLEASE NOTE

When cooking the multitude of recipes in our test kitchens for this book, my team and I used a variety of slow cookers. Naturally we all owned different models, it was interesting the variations to recipes and foods that resulted. In one instance, more liquid evaporated from the cooker leaving less sauce than when the same dish was prepared in a different model. The dish was still delicious but required the addition of a little more liquid before serving.

Because all slow cookers are not created equally, you will still need to monitor. Don't just rely on the stated cook times for a recipe until you know how your slow cooker performs. Use these recipes as guides, but use your instinct as well; combined you will have success.

# REASONS TO LOVE YOUR SLOW COOKER

1. ***SAVES TIME.*** The slow cooker is the perfect solution for all busy people. You simply place the ingredients into the cooker, switch it on to cook anywhere from 4 to 8 hours and *VOILA* - dinner is done! The interesting paradox about slow cooking is that while the food takes longer to cook, the cook has more free time. It's such a liberating feeling to put dinner on in the morning and know it'll be ready when you are.

2. ***SAVES MONEY.*** IT'S TRUE, you save money on electricity because it costs less to run a slow cooker for 6 to 8 hours than an oven for 1 hour. You also save by purchasing less expensive cuts of meat. There's no need to splurge on extra-tender (and extra-pricey) filet mignon when using a slow cooker. The slightly tougher, rougher, and "less desirable" (cheaper) cuts of meat are perfect for slow cookers since the long and low-temperature cooking technique softens them right up.

3. ***SAVES ENERGY.*** The most annoying and draining task in the kitchen – BAR NONE – is washing up! The slow cooker is ideal for those who lack a dishwasher or the energy to wash a sink load of pots and pans right after dinner (ME). With just one large pot to wash you will use less water, less soap, less electricity and most importantly less elbow grease. Slow cooking is really one pot cooking at it's best.

4. ***CREATES ROBUST FLAVOURS & WHOLESOME MEALS.*** Slow cooking is said to protect the enzymes and nutrients in food and doesn't destroy them in the same way as boiling, roasting or frying does. Slow cooker recipes will rarely call for added oils or fats, so most recipes will be lower fat and full of the wonderful flavours of your chosen ingredients.

5. ***FEEDS LARGE AMOUNTS OF PEOPLE.*** When you need to feed a crowd, your slow cooker is indispensable. Turn it into a fondue pot, soup tureen; slowly cook a pork shoulder on game nights, or shanks for a dinner party. The possibilities are effortlessly and deliciously endless. A slow cooked meal can also be easily transported to a party or gathering. Just let it cool slightly, keep it covered and you can refrigerate or serve straight from the bowl.

6. ***EVEN BETTER THE NEXT DAY.*** Slow cookers offer the ability to increase quantities and batch cook with ease. Anything made will have even more depth of flavour as leftovers; perfect for lunchboxes the next day or to transform into another incredible family meal.

7. ***VEGGIE SMUGGLER.*** I will always add veggies to my slow cooker for extra nutrients and flavour. You can save even more money and reduce your grocery waste, if you use up the flat and forgotten veggies hiding in your crisper or in cans in your pantry.

8. Slow cooking is perfect for people with ***INFLAMMATORY BOWEL DISEASES*** like Crohn's or Colitis, irritable bowel syndrome (IBS), or anyone with inflammation in the gut as the cooking process helps to break down the foods, so that your digestive system doesn't have to do all the work.

9. ***USE YOUR SLOW COOKER ALL YEAR ROUND.*** We might associate warm, comforting hot meals with wintertime, but the beauty of slow cookers is that you can use them any time of year. The joy of using one in the summer is that it eliminates the need to use the oven, reducing the discomfort of making an already hot home, hotter.

# SENSATIONAL SLOW COOKER TIPS

### Lightly spray with olive oil

Lightly spray the inside of the slow cooker with non-stick cooking spray or line with baking paper. This will make clean up a breeze and extend the life of your cooker bowl. Simply make our own spray oil by filling a reusable spray bottle with olive oil.

### Don't use lean cuts of meat

Slow cookers work best with fatty or tougher cuts of meat. It is the fat that keeps the meat moist, and results in deliciously tender meat when cooked low and slow. An even bigger bonus, is that generally the fattier cuts of meat are cheaper and often on sale. The only exception to this rule is with beef or lamb mince; I do use lean mince when slow cooking as you'll see in the recipes where this ingredient is included.

### Know when to go HIGH & when to go LOW

Use the HIGH setting if you need to cook a tenderer cut of meat relatively quickly. But for tougher cuts, it's best to use the LOW setting and cook longer to allow time for its fat to release and the meat to grow tender.

### No Peeking

Don't be tempted to lift the lid often. The steam generated during slow cooking is part of the cooking medium. Opening the lid will release this steam, decrease the inside temperature and increase cooking time by 15 to 20 minutes. Only open 60 to 30 minutes prior to the low end of the cooking time to check progress or to turn into the sauce.

### Use less liquid

Because the slow cooker generates steam that doesn't escape, there will be more liquid in the food when it's finished cooking, than when it started. If you create or adapt a recipe for the slow cooker, decrease (by as much as half) the amount of liquid you normally use in the dish. Many people think that meat and vegetables have to be completely covered in liquid to slow cook it, when in fact they need very little liquid. If you find the end result has far too much liquid, next time reduce the amount you add in the first place or look further for the thickening tips.

## The Tea Towel Tip

I first read about this tip years ago; the rationale is that by placing a tea towel between the lid and top of the slow cooker, it prevents the condensation that forms on the inside of the lid from dripping back down onto the food. I use this method any time I use the slow cooker for a recipe that needs to stay dry; usually when I'm baking cakes and breads.

## Cornflour Paste

To thicken the many flavourful gravies that will result; make a simple cornflour paste by whisking together 2 tbsp. cornflour in 4 tbsp. cold water until it becomes a nice, smooth paste. Pour the runny gravy from the slow cooker into a large non-stick frying pan and bring to a gentle boil. Gradually add the cornflour paste whisking until nice and smooth and thick.

## The Grated Tattie Tip

I love this tip; grate 1 to 2 raw potatoes (Idaho or Russet are high in starch and low in moisture) and add them to the slow cooker about 30 to 45 minutes before serving. This will thicken the dish and, like the cornflour paste, is a fabulous gluten free option if ever you need it.

## Savour the Flavour

Whole spices and herbs like cinnamon sticks, bay leaves, caraway seeds, peppercorns, rosemary and garlic will give intense flavour to a dish that cooks for several hours, so be careful not to overdo them. For fresher flavours, add soft herbs e.g. parsley, basil and coriander about 10 minutes before the meal is ready. When cooked for long periods of time, fresh herbs will lose their flavours. Similarly, when adding dairy, like cream, add at the very end to prevent curdling.

## TRIM the FAT

Although we just said that it's the fat that adds the flavour and while that is 100% true, too much fat left on the meat will result in an unpleasant texture, or having to skim lots of fat at the end of cooking. When making all the recipes, I trimmed excess amounts of fat for maximum results.

## Layering

Your slow cooker heat source is in the base so nestle the foods that will take longest to cook into the cooker first. Thick, dense vegetables, large pieces of meat and meat with bones - they go in first. Any delicate, quick cooking vegetables should be layered on top or added in the last 30 minutes of cooking time.

# THE BEST CUTS OF MEAT FOR SLOW COOKING

**What we love most about our slow cookers are their ability to turn the cheapest cuts of meat into tender morsels that just melt in your mouth. If you're unsure what cuts of meat to look for, then this handy guide will help you select the best cut every time.**

## Beef in the slow cooker

From stews to curries, chilli to casseroles, beef is arguably the most versatile meat for slow cooking, and a great choice to keep in the freezer ready to transform into these delicious meals. The very best beef cuts to keep on hand to slow cook are blade steak, chuck steak, round steak, silverside, skirt steak, shin (gravy) beef, sausages and topside.

## Lamb in the slow cooker

A perfect addition to the slow cooker, lamb cuts turn meltingly tender and flavoursome when left to slowly bubble away. When choosing a slow cooker lamb recipe, pick up the following cuts for best results: Boneless shoulder, boneless forequarter, leg roasts, shanks, neck chops and sausages.

## Pork in the slow cooker

Pork makes a fabulous addition to a slow cooked meal, adding sweetness and depth to a range of dishes. It's a particularly great addition to bean and sausage dishes. When choosing pork cuts to slow cook opt for the following: Pork shoulder, pork chops, pork neck, bone-in roasts, ribs, ham hocks and sausages.

## Chicken in the slow cooker

Although not as popular in slow cooked dishes as red meat, chicken makes a perfect addition to many classics, especially curries and stews. When choosing chicken cuts to slow cook, opt for bone-in to boost flavour and keep the meat moist. Here are some of the best cuts; thigh pieces (skinless, boneless and bone-in), drumsticks or Marylands. If using breast, cook on low and cook it whole, to prevent it drying out.

## Veal in the slow cooker

One of the best, and most under-rated meats for the pot is veal. Perhaps the most-popular veal recipe of all is slow-cooked Osso Bucco. When choosing a veal cut to slow cook opt for sliced shin, shoulder or shanks.

# SLOW COOKER FOOD WEIGHTS & COOK TIMES

| | Weight | Low | High |
|---|---|---|---|
| Beef – Mince | 500g – 1kg | 6 – 8 hours | |
| Beef – Roast | 1.5kg | 6 – 8 hours | 4 – 6 hours |
| Beef – Steak (Blade, BBQ) | 250g each | 3 – 4 hours | 2 hours |
| Beef – Stewing Meat (Chuck, Blade) | 1.5kg | 6 – 8 hours | 4 – 5 hours |
| Beef – Sausages | 1kg | 4 hours | |
| Poultry – Breast | 500g – 1kg | 2 – 3 hours | |
| Poultry – Drumstick | 1 – 1.5kg | 3 – 4 hours | 1.5 – 2 hours |
| Poultry – Mince | 500g – 1kg | 5 – 7 hours | |
| Poultry – Thigh Cutlet | 1kg | 4 – 5 hours | |
| Lamb – Roast | 1.5 – 2kg | 8 hours | 4 – 6 hours |
| Lamb – Chops (Forequarter) | 1.5kg | 5 – 6 hours | 3 – 4 hours |
| Lamb – Shanks | 2kg | 6 – 8 hours | 4 hours |
| Pork – Shoulder | 1.5 – 2kg | 8 hours | |
| Pork – Chops (Forequarter) | 1kg | 5 – 6 hours | 3 – 4 hours |

**NOTE:** Cooking times may vary depending on the several factors including your individual appliance, how many times you remove the lid, if your meat is whole or sliced and the thickness of your cut. Monitor; use these tried and tested recipes and your instinct. Combining both of those will result in deliciously tender meals for the whole family.

**BEEF**

Beef cooked in a slow cooker creates a richness of flavour that cannot be matched with any other method of cooking. Try these deliciously tender beef casseroles, soups & stews.

# SERVES 4

There are few foods as comforting as a juicy, tender meatball and cooked slowly in this yummy, flavourful sauce. These are just... *AMAZING!*

## INGREDIENTS

- 500g lean beef mince
- 2 eggs, beaten
- 4 tbsp. uncooked rice
- 2 x 420g can condensed tomato soup

## + GOURMET GARDEN

- 2 tbsp. Gourmet Garden Lightly Dried Mixed Herbs
- 1 tbsp. Gourmet Garden Garlic Stir-In Paste

## METHOD

1. Combine all ingredients except for the soup, and season with sea salt and cracked pepper.

2. Roll into meatballs and place in the slow cooker.

3. Pour the soup over the meatballs.

4. Swirl ½ cup water around the first empty can of soup, then pour that into the second empty can of soup again swirling to remove all the soup, add, stirring gently to coat the meatballs.

5. Cover and cook on LOW for 4 to 5 hours or HIGH for 2 to 3 or until rice is tender and poking out of the yummy meatballs.

# BEER & BEEF SLIDERS
## SERVES 4

## INGREDIENTS

- 1kg topside beef roast (chuck is also fine)
- ⅓ cup loosely packed brown sugar
- 1 tsp. smoked paprika
- 1 cup beer

## + GOURMET GARDEN

- 1 tbsp. Gourmet Garden Garlic Stir-In Paste
- 2 tsp. Gourmet Garden Mild Chilli Stir-In Paste

## METHOD

1. Place the beef in the slow cooker.

2. Brush with garlic and chilli, then sprinkle with brown sugar and paprika.

3. Add the beer.

4. Cover and cook on LOW for 8 hours or until the beef is tender.

5. Use two forks to shred and pull the beef apart.

6. Leave sit in the delicious sauce for at least 15 minutes.

**OPTIONAL:** Serve piled onto crusty bread rolls with a ring of tomato, onion and a fresh leaf of lettuce.

# BEEF STROGANOFF
## SERVES 4

Quick, easy, creamy stroganoff for fellow slow cooker fans.

## INGREDIENTS

- 600g chuck beef, diced
- 35g packet beef stroganoff seasoning
- 16 button mushrooms, halved
- 100g cream cheese, softened

## + GOURMET GARDEN

- 1 tbsp. Gourmet Garden Garlic Stir-In Paste
- 1 tbsp. Gourmet Garden Chives Stir-In Paste

## METHOD

1. Place the beef in the slow cooker.

2. In a small jug whisk together the stroganoff seasoning, ½ cup of water and garlic.

3. Cook on LOW for 6 to 8 hours, or HIGH for 3 to 4 hours.

4. Stir in the mushrooms 1 hour before serving and cream cheese and chives 30 minutes beforehand, mixing through gently.

5. Season to taste before serving.

**OPTIONAL:** Serve this yummy meal with rice to soak up the delicious sauce that results.

# BEEF WITH CHILLI PLUM SAUCE

## SERVES 4

When you want to make something popular, this fits the bill beautifully. I use SPC plum sauce; in addition to the natural sweetness of plums it is lightly infused with delicate spices that are just divine when mixed with mustard and chilli.

## INGREDIENTS

- ¾ cup plum sauce
- 1 tbsp. English mustard
- 800g BBQ steak, cut into 2cm thick strips
- ⅓ cup sultanas (or raisins)

## + GOURMET GARDEN

- 1 tbsp. Gourmet Garden Lightly Dried Chilli

## METHOD

1. Combine plum sauce, mustard and chilli (you may want to reduce the chilli if cooking for children) in a large bowl.

2. Add the beef and toss to coat well.

3. Place the beef into the slow cooker.

4. Stir in the sultanas, season with sea salt and cracked pepper.

5. Cover and cook on LOW for 3 hours or until the meat is deliciously tender.

**OPTIONAL:** Serve with fluffy rice and garnish with Gourmet Garden Lightly Dried Parsley.

# BRAISED STEAK & ONIONS
## SERVES 6

A good ole, traditional meal for those busy days when you need your slow cooker to do all the work. Don't let anyone tell you that you can't do steak in a slow cooker; you can, this dish is living proof.

## INGREDIENTS

- 6 x 250g blade steak
- 2 brown onions, peeled and quartered
- 2 tbsp. Worcestershire sauce
- 1 cup BBQ sauce

## + GOURMET GARDEN

- 1 tbsp. Gourmet Garden Garlic Stir-In Paste

## METHOD

1. Season the steaks with sea salt and cracked pepper and nestle into the slow cooker.

2. Add the onions.

3. In a small bowl, mix together remaining ingredients and pour over the beef.

4. Cover and cook on LOW for 3 to 4 hours or HIGH for 2 hours.

**OPTIONAL:** Delicious served with sautéed cabbage or Brussels sprouts and carrots.

BOLOG
SAUCE

# SERVES 4

*MAKE DOUBLE...* As this is fabulous the next day served piled on a baked potato with either grated cheese on top, or with a dollop of sour cream garnished with parsley. Or simply spread leftover onto a sheet of puff pastry sprinkled with baby spinach and grated Parmesan. Season. Roll. Slice. Bake. Devour!

## INGREDIENTS

- 500g lean beef mince
- 1 large brown onion, diced
- 425g can whole tomatoes with garlic
- 1 tsp. beef stock powder

## + GOURMET GARDEN

- 2 tbsp. Gourmet Garden Lightly Dried Mixed Herbs
- 1 tbsp. Gourmet Garden Lightly Dried Parsley

## METHOD

1. Combine all ingredients (except parsley) in the slow cooker.
2. Cover and cook on LOW for 6 hours or on HIGH for 3 hours.
3. In the last 10 minutes, stir in the parsley.
4. Season to taste and serve with your family's favourite pasta.

**OPTIONAL:** This is a great veggie smuggler, so add whatever veggies you have to the yummy sauce.

BUTTER
ROAST

# SERVES 8

## INGREDIENTS

- 2kg beef roast
- ¾ cup buttermilk
- 35g French onion soup mix

## + GOURMET GARDEN

- 1 tbsp. Gourmet Garden Thyme Stir-In Paste

## METHOD

1. Trim all visible fat from the meat, and then place in the slow cooker.
2. Rub the meat with thyme and season generously with cracked pepper.
3. Mix together buttermilk and soup mix; pour over the roast.
4. Cook on LOW for 6 hours.
5. At the end of 6 hours remove the meat, set aside and rest for 10 minutes.
6. Slice the succulent meat and serve drizzled with the gravy that results.

**OPTIONAL:** The gravy is quite runny; to reduce you may want to create a cornflour paste by mixing 2 tbsp. cornflour with 4 tbsp. cold water. Once smooth, pour the gravy into a large non-stick frying pan over a high heat and gradually add the paste, stirring to combine and thicken.

# MILK
## *with Thyme Infused Gravy*

CHILLI
CON CA

# SERVES 4

A perfect meal ideal for the larger family – just double the batch to feed more.
If leftovers, freeze the extra and use it as a filling for tacos, or a tortilla stack or
as a topping on a baked potato served with a dollop of sour cream mixed with
Gourmet Garden Chives Stir-In Paste.

## INGREDIENTS

- 500g lean beef mince
- 35g packet chilli con carne seasoning
- 410g can diced tomatoes
- 420g can red kidney beans, rinsed

## + GOURMET GARDEN

- 1 tbsp. Gourmet Garden Lightly Dried Chilli
- 1 tbsp. Gourmet Garden Garlic Stir-In Paste
- 1 tbsp. Gourmet Garden Lightly Dried Coriander

## METHOD

1. Place all the ingredients (except the coriander) in the slow cooker and season with cracked pepper.

2. Cook on LOW for 6 to 8 hours.

3. In the last 10 minutes, stir in the coriander.

**OPTIONAL:** Serve over fluffy rice, with a dollop of sour cream and a sprinkle of freshly chopped shallots.

# COFFEE SLOW COOKED BEEF WITH GARLIC & CHILLI

## SERVES 8

## INGREDIENTS

- 2kg chuck roast. trimmed of any visible fat
- 1 cup double strength coffee
- 2 tbsp. cornflour

### + GOURMET GARDEN

- 2 tbsp. Gourmet Garden Garlic Stir-In Paste
- 1 tbsp. Gourmet Garden Lightly Dried Chilli

## METHOD

1. Place the meat in the slow cooker.

2. Rub with garlic, sprinkle with chilli and season generously with sea salt and cracked pepper.

3. Pour the coffee over the meat.

4. Cook on LOW for 6 to 8 hours.

5. When the roast is done, remove from slow cooker, cover with foil and rest for 10 minutes before slicing.

6. In a small bowl, whisk the cornflour with 4 tbsp. cold water to create a smooth paste.

7. Pour the slow cooker juices into a large frying pan and bring to a gentle boil.

8. Gradually add the cornflour paste, stirring constantly until thickened.

9. Season to taste, with coffee granules, sea salt and cracked pepper.

10. Serve this yummy gravy over the sliced beef.

**OPTIONAL:** Mashed sweet potato and steamed broccolini make a lovely accompaniment with the smokey, spicy flavours of the beef.

# CREAMY GARLIC STEAK DIANE

## SERVES 6

A throw back to the 70's, where no dinner party would be complete without a classic Steak Diane served with creamy mashed potatoes and steamed green beans...
And guess what? It's still as delightful as ever.

## INGREDIENTS

- 6 x 200g cuts of budget round steak
- ¼ cup Worcestershire sauce
- ¼ cup brandy
- ¼ cup thickened cream

## + GOURMET GARDEN

- 1 tbsp. Gourmet Garden Garlic Stir-In Paste

## METHOD

1. Place the steaks in the slow cooker and rub with garlic and season with sea salt and cracked pepper.

2. Pour over the Worcestershire sauce and brandy.

3. Cover and cook on LOW for 6 hours.

4. Remove steaks, cover with foil and let sit for 5 minutes.

5. Pour the slow cooker juices into a large frying pan, bringing to a gentle boil.

6. Gradually whisk in the cream.

7. Continue to boil gently until reduced to desired consistency.

8. Season to taste and serve drizzled over the deliciously tender steaks.

EASIES
BEEF EV

# SERVES 6

## INGREDIENTS

- 1kg chuck roast, trimmed of any visible fat
- 35g packet French onion soup
- 420g can condensed mushroom soup

## + GOURMET GARDEN

- 1 tbsp. Gourmet Garden Parsley Stir-In Paste

## METHOD

1. Place the beef in the slow cooker.
2. Whisk together the two soups.
3. Pour over the beef and season with cracked pepper.
4. Cook on LOW for 6 to 8 hours.
5. In the last 10 minutes, stir in the parsley.
6. Slice and serve with the flavourful gravy that will inevitably lift everything else on the plate; it's wonderful.

ROAST

ER

GINGER
SILVERS

# SERVES 8

*DID YOU KNOW* that ginger is considered one of the world's healthiest foods? Aromatic and spicy, ginger adds a gorgeous flavour to this incredibly easy dish.

## INGREDIENTS

- 2.5kg silverside, fat removed, rinsed
- 1.25 litres ginger ale

## + GOURMET GARDEN

- 2 tbsp. Gourmet Garden Lightly Dried Ginger

## METHOD

1. Pop the meat into the slow cooker.
2. Sprinkle with ginger and season with cracked pepper.
3. Pour over ginger ale.
4. Cover and cook on LOW for 6 to 8 hours or until silverside is soft to slice and succulent.

**OPTIONAL:** Serve with your favourite mustard or this deliciously **Easy White Sauce:** In a medium saucepan over a moderate heat melt 50g butter. Stir in 2 tbsp. plain four and mix to combine. Remove from heat, gradually add 2 cups of milk, stirring, until smooth. Return to heat, stirring until nice and thick. Stir in 2 tsp. wholegrain mustard and 2 tbsp. parsley. Season to taste.

NFUSED
IDE

# HEALTHY OSSO BUCCO

## SERVES 4

'Osso Bucco' is an Italian dish made of shin or veal containing marrowbone stewed in wine with vegetables. However our 'healthy' version substitutes the wine for chopped tomatoes; use whatever takes your fancy.

## INGREDIENTS

- 4 French-trimmed beef or veal shanks
- 2 large carrots, cut into thick rounds
- 420g can cannellini beans, drained, rinsed
- 410g can chopped tomatoes with roasted capsicum

## + GOURMET GARDEN

- 2 tbsp. Gourmet Garden Thyme Stir-In Paste

## METHOD

1. Place the shanks in the slow cooker.

2. Coat with thyme and season generously with sea salt and cracked pepper.

3. Add the carrots, then the cannellini beans.

4. Pour over the tomatoes with roasted capsicum.

5. Swirl ½ cup water around the empty can of tomatoes to remove all the sauce and add.

6. Cover and cook on LOW for 6 to 8 hours or until the meat is tender.

7. Season to taste.

# ITALIAN BEEF & RED WINE CASSEROLE
## SERVES 6

Ten minutes of prep time is all you need for this rich, but simple recipe.

## INGREDIENTS

- ½ cup plain flour
- 1kg chuck steak (beef), cut into pieces
- 1 cup red wine
- 410g can crushed tomatoes with garlic

## + GOURMET GARDEN

- 2 tbsp. Gourmet Garden Lightly Dried Mixed Herbs

## METHOD

1. Into a plastic bag, spoon the flour and season generously with sea salt and cracked pepper.

2. Add the steak and shake to coat.

3. Place the dusted steak into the slow cooker.

4. Add the red wine, tomatoes and mixed herbs and stir to combine.

5. Cook on LOW for 6 hours.

**OPTIONAL:** Serve this sprinkled with a **Quick Gremolata:** Simply combine ⅓ cup chopped flat leaf parsley, 2 tsp. lemon zest and 1 tsp. Gourmet Garden Garlic Stir-In Paste.

MAGIC
MEALS

# SERVES 6

It's the fresh flavours of Gourmet Garden's Mediterranean Seasoning, the perfect blend of basil, oregano, garlic and capsicum that make this meatloaf 'magic'.

## INGREDIENTS

- ¼ cup pizza paste (+1 tbsp. for basting)
- 500g beef mince
- 1 cup grated Mozzarella cheese
- 1 egg

## + GOURMET GARDEN

- 1 tbsp. Gourmet Garden Lightly Dried Parsley
- 2 tbsp. Gourmet Garden Mediterranean Stir-In Seasoning

## METHOD

1. Line a loaf tin with baking paper.

2. Baste the base with the extra tablespoon of pizza paste, then sprinkle with parsley.

3. In a large mixing bowl, combine all other ingredients, season generously with sea salt and cracked pepper.

4. Press the mixture into the prepared tin.

5. Place the tin into the slow cooker, lay a tea towel under the lid (the tea towel lies between the slow cooker and the lid and acts to absorb condensation and stop it dripping down into the food cooking inside).

6. Cover and cook on LOW for 6 to 7 hours or HIGH for 3 to 4 hours.

OPTIONAL: Add 1 cup of seasoned breadcrumbs to the mixture for extra bulk.
Use any leftovers on bread rolls the next day to create **"Scrumptious Meatloaf Subs."**

# MONGOLIAN BEEF
## SERVES 4

To make this yummy dish I asked my gorgeous butcher to cut some cheap, BBQ steak into even strips; they worked beautifully.

---

### INGREDIENTS

- 750g BBQ steak, cut into 2cm thick slices
- 4 shallots, sliced
- ½ cup ketjap manis (sweet soy sauce)
- ½ cup raw cashews

### + GOURMET GARDEN

- 1 tsp. Gourmet Garden Garlic Stir-In Paste
- 1 tsp. Gourmet Garden Ginger Stir-In Paste

### METHOD

1. Place the beef in a slow cooker.
2. Add the shallots.
3. In a small bowl, mix together the ketjap manis, ginger and garlic with 2 tbsp. water.
4. Pour over the meat and stir to coat.
5. Cover and cook on LOW for 3 hours or until the beef is deliciously tender.
6. With 10 minutes to go, stir through the cashews.

**OPTIONAL:** Serve over basmati rice with additional thinly sliced shallots; drizzled with the deliciously sweet jus that remains.

# SAUSAGES WITH ONION GRAVY

## SERVES 4

---

## INGREDIENTS

- 2 large brown onions, peeled and sliced into rings
- 1 cup beef stock
- 3 tbsp. cornflour
- 8 thin beef sausages

## + GOURMET GARDEN

- 1 tbsp, Gourmet Garden Rosemary Stir-In Paste
- 1 tbsp. Gourmet Garden Garlic Stir-In Paste

## METHOD

1. Place the onions in the base of a slow cooker.

2. In a jug, combine stock, cornflour, rosemary and garlic and whisk to a smooth consistency.

3. Pour over the onions.

4. Add the sausages.

5. Cover and cook on LOW for 6 hours.

6. When finished cooking, remove sausages and place on serving plates, spoon over the tasty gravy.

**OPTIONAL:** Add two or three roughly chopped carrots to the mix; they never tasted so good. Serve with creamy mashed potatoes and peas.

# CKEN

Never cook chicken with its skin on. Usually, we love chicken skin, it crisps up so beautifully when fried or sautéed. But in a slow cooker, where things stew instead of sear, the skin tends to turn rubbery. Simply buy your chicken skinless or remove excess skin because chicken in a slow cooker will not only fill your home with the aroma of a delicious meal, but produces a tasty, moist dinner the whole family can enjoy.

# APRICOT CHILLI CHICKEN
## SERVES 6

### INGREDIENTS

- 35g packet of French onion soup mix
- 400ml can apricot nectar
- 1 onion, peeled and sliced
- 1kg boneless, skinless chicken thighs

### + GOURMET GARDEN

- 1 tbsp. Gourmet Garden Chilli Stir-In Paste
- 1 tbsp. Gourmet Garden Lightly Dried Coriander

### METHOD

1. Combine French onion soup, apricot nectar and chilli in the slow cooker.

2. Add the onion and chicken, then stir to coat.

3. Cover and cook on LOW for 3 to 4 hours.

4. In the last 10 minutes, stir through the coriander .

**OPTIONAL:** If too runny, reduce this sauce by creating a cornflour paste. Mix 2 tbsp. cornflour with 4 tbsp. cold water. Once smooth, pour the sauce into a large non-stick frying pan over a high heat and gradually add the paste, stirring until nice and thick.

# CHICKEN & JARLSBERG CASSEROLE

## SERVES 6

This is such an easy recipe to assemble and one of my favourites for a casual weekend dinner with family and friends.

## INGREDIENTS

- 6 boneless, skinless chicken breast halves
- 6 slices Jarlsberg cheese
- 420g can condensed cream of chicken soup

## + GOURMET GARDEN

- 1 tbsp. Gourmet Garden Lightly Dried Parsley

## METHOD

1. Place the chicken in a slow cooker and cover with cheese.

2. Spoon the soup over the chicken and season with cracked pepper.

3. Cook on LOW for 4 hours.

4. Serve sprinkled with parsley.

OPTIONAL: As with p.40, if this sauce is a little too runny, simply thicken with a cornflour paste.

CHICKEN CACCIA

# SERVES 6

## INGREDIENTS

- 6 skinless, chicken thigh cutlets (bone-in)
- 100g pitted Kalamata olives
- 1 red capsicum, sliced
- 700g jar Arrabbiata sauce

## + GOURMET GARDEN

- 1 tbsp. Gourmet Garden Chilli Stir-In Paste
- 1 tbsp. Gourmet Garden Basil Stir-In Paste
- 1 tbsp. Gourmet Garden Lightly Dried Parsley

## METHOD

1. Place the chicken in the slow cooker.
2. Surround with olives and capsicums.
3. In a large bowl, mix together Arrabbiata sauce, chilli and basil.
4. Pour the sauce over chicken and vegetables, stirring to coat well.
5. Cook on LOW for 4 to 5 hours.
6. Season to taste with parsley, sea salt and pepper.

**OPTIONAL:** Serve with creamy mashed potato and steamed greens.

# CHICKEN FAJITAS

## SERVES 4

---

## INGREDIENTS

- 500g boneless, skinless chicken breast halves
- 410g can crushed tomatoes
- 35g packet Reduced Salt Taco seasoning
- 2 generous tbsp. cream cheese

## + GOURMET GARDEN

- 1 tbsp. Gourmet Garden Coriander Stir-In Paste

## METHOD

1. Place the chicken in the slow cooker.

2. In a bowl, mix together tomatoes and taco seasoning.

3. Pour over chicken.

4. Cover and cook on LOW for 3 to 4 hours or until the meat shreds effortlessly when pulled with two forks.

5. Add the cream cheese and coriander and stir well to combine.

6. Rest for 10 minutes to thicken a little before serving.

**OPTIONAL:** Serve over tortillas with your choice of toppings; grated cheese, finely diced tomatoes, red onions and jalapeños, guacamole, sour cream etc.

# CHICKEN LASAGNE
## SERVES 4

---

## INGREDIENTS

- 500g jar chunky vegetable and tomato pasta sauce
- 600g chicken tenderloins
- 1½ cups grated Mozzarella cheese
- 8 lasagne sheets, broken up

## + GOURMET GARDEN

- 2 tbsp. Gourmet Garden Lightly Dried Mixed Herbs

## METHOD

1. Line the bowl of a slow cooker with baking paper.

2. Spread the base with pasta sauce, a layer of chicken and top with cheese.

3. Layer across lasagne sheet pieces and a sprinkle of mixed herbs.

4. Repeat layers until chicken is used, finishing the top layer with sauce, cheese and mixed herbs.

5. Cover and cook on LOW for 2 to 3 hours.

6. Serve garnished with mixed herbs, sea salt and cracked pepper.

**OPTIONAL:** Add vegetables such as baby spinach, grated carrots and or zucchini to the layers.

COUNTRY CHICKEN CASSERO

# SERVES 4

On a winter's evening there is surely nothing better than coming home from a long day at work to find a bubbling casserole ready to eat.

## INGREDIENTS

- 8 boneless, skinless chicken pieces (mixed)
- 6 slices short cut bacon, chopped & lightly sautéed
- 4 stalks celery, chopped
- 420g can condensed cream of chicken soup

## + GOURMET GARDEN

- 1 to 2 tbsp. Gourmet Garden Chives Stir-In Paste

## METHOD

1. Place the chicken in the slow cooker.

2. Season with cracked pepper.

3. Top with bacon, celery and soup.

4. Cover and cook on LOW for 4 to 5 hours or until the chicken is cooked.

5. With 10 minutes to go, remove lid, stir in chives and season to taste.

OPTIONAL: Eat half and use the leftovers in little **Chicken Pot Pies;** simply fill a ramekin with the leftover casserole and top with a round of puff pastry. Bake in a hot oven for 20 minutes or until pastry is puffed and golden.

& CHIVE
LE

# SERVES 6

The fresh flavours of Italy are easily conjured with Gourmet Garden's Lightly Dried Mixed Herbs. It has the perfect blend of basil, oregano and parsley to give you tasty Italian inspired meals.

## INGREDIENTS

- 800g chicken mince
- 1 cup freshly grated breadcrumbs
  (I used 4 slices wholemeal bread)
- 80g semi dried tomatoes
- 80g feta cheese

## + GOURMET GARDEN

- 3 tbsp. Gourmet Garden Lightly Dried Mixed Herbs

## METHOD

1. In a large bowl mix the chicken mince, breadcrumbs and mixed herbs.
2. Season generously with sea salt and cracked pepper.
3. On a large piece of baking paper, flatten the mince mixture into a rectangular shape, 2cm thick.
4. Place the tomatoes and crumble the feta over the centre of the mince and roll up into a log.
5. Lay the log into a slow cooker.
6. Cook on LOW for 6 to 7 hours or HIGH for 3 to 4 hours.
7. Remove and rest for 10 minutes before slicing into rounds to serve.

# FIESTA CHICKEN
## SERVES 6

This dish is like a festival on a plate (hence the name). It's quick, easy and super delicious, there is absolutely nothing about it not to love.

## INGREDIENTS

- 1kg skinless chicken pieces (mixed)
- 500g jar apricot jam

## + GOURMET GARDEN

- 2 tbsp. Gourmet Garden Ginger Stir-In Paste

## METHOD

1. Place the chicken in a slow cooker.
2. Combine the jam and ginger, then spoon over the chicken.
3. Roll the chicken to coat.
4. Season with sea salt and cracked pepper.
5. Cover and cook on LOW for 4 to 5 hours or until the chicken is cooked.

**OPTIONAL:** In a non-stick frying pan pour the yummy sauce from the cooker and over a moderate heat reduce to desired consistency. Nestle the chicken back into the sauce and toss to coat. Serve with a lightly, fluffy rice to soak up the sweet syrup.

# HONEY MUSTARD & DILL CHICKEN
## SERVES 6

The addition of dill gives this dish a really lovely flavour; and we all know that *FLAVOUR* is the most important ingredient in any dish.

## INGREDIENTS

- 6 chicken thigh cutlets (bone-in)
- ¼ cup Dijon mustard
- ½ cup honey

## + GOURMET GARDEN

- 1 tbsp. Gourmet Garden Dill Stir-In Paste

## METHOD

1. Place the chicken in a slow cooker.

2. Combine remaining ingredients in a bowl with 2 tbsp. warm water.

3. Pour the mixture over the chicken, turning the chicken to coat well.

4. Season with sea salt and cracked pepper.

5. Cover and cook on LOW for 4 to 5 hours.

**OPTIONAL:** The yummy sauce is quite runny so to reduce, you may want to create a cornflour paste by mixing 2 tbsp. cornflour with 4 tbsp. cold water. Once smooth, pour the honey mustard sauce into a large non-stick frying pan over a high heat and gradually add the paste, stirring to combine and thicken. Serve the chicken drizzled with sauce, and with couscous or rice and a freshly prepared garden salad.

# MOROCCAN SWEET & SPICY CHICKEN

## SERVES 6

Coriander, ginger, garlic and cumin merge into one delicious seasoning to add the authentic flavour of Morocco in this simple dish.

## INGREDIENTS

- 1 onion, peeled and sliced
- 6 skinless, chicken thigh cutlets (bone-in)
- 410g can diced tomatoes with garlic
- ½ cup raisins

## + GOURMET GARDEN

- 2 tbsp. Gourmet Garden Moroccan Stir-In Seasoning

## METHOD

1. Into the slow cooker, place the onion.

2. Add the chicken, tomatoes, raisins and Moroccan Seasoning.

3. Stir to combine the sauces.

4. Cover and cook on LOW for 4 to 5 hours or until the chicken is tender.

5. Season to taste before serving.

# SATAY CHICKEN

## SERVES 4

I'm naturally drawn to anything Satay because of the lightly spiced peanut flavours and texture; the combination is sensational.

## INGREDIENTS

- 1kg boneless, skinless chicken thighs
- ½ cup crunchy peanut butter
- 2 tbsp. lime juice and zest
- ¼ cup ketjap manis (sweet soy sauce)

## + GOURMET GARDEN

- 1 tsp. Gourmet Garden Lightly Dried Ginger
- 1 tbsp. Gourmet Garden Thai Stir-In Seasoning

## METHOD

1. Place the chicken in a slow cooker.

2. In a small mixing bowl, stir together remaining ingredients.

3. Pour over the chicken, turning to coat well.

4. Cover and cook on LOW for 3 to 4 hours or until the meat is so tender it melts in your mouth.

**OPTIONAL:** Serve in bowls with brown rice and steamed Asian vegetables; and for a little extra crunch scatter over chopped peanuts.

PICANT
CHICKE

# SERVES 6

Picante in Spanish means 'spicy,' and this dish is that. But it's a pleasant sweet spiciness that your entire family will love.

## INGREDIENTS

- 2 cups salsa
- ⅓ cup brown sugar
- 2 tbsp. Dijon mustard
- 6 boneless, skinless chicken breast halves

## + GOURMET GARDEN

- 2 tsp. Gourmet Garden Chilli Stir-In Paste
- 1 tbsp. Gourmet Garden Garlic Stir-In Paste

## METHOD

1. Combine salsa, sugar, mustard, chilli and garlic in the slow cooker.

2. Add the chicken, turning to coat well.

3. Cover and cook on LOW for 2 to 3 hours.

**OPTIONAL:** Add strips of red capsicum before baking for added colour and flavour and serve over rice for dinner, then shred for yummy wraps the next day for lunch.

# STICKY CHICKEN DRUMMETTES
## SERVES 8

With over 24 million views on YouTube, this is a winner, winner chicken dinner!

## INGREDIENTS

- 2kg chicken drummettes
- 1 cup BBQ sauce (+ 2 tbsp. for basting)
- 1 cup sarsparilla
- 2 tbsp. brown sugar

## + GOURMET GARDEN

- 2 tsp. Gourmet Garden Chilli Stir-In Paste
- 1 tbsp. Gourmet Garden Garlic Stir-In Paste

## METHOD

1. Place the chicken, 1 cup BBQ sauce, sarsaparilla, chilli and garlic into the slow cooker.

2. Stir to completely coat.

3. Cover and cook on LOW for 3 to 4 hours.

4. Line a baking tray with baking paper.

5. Remove the chicken and place on the prepared tray.

6. Brush with 1 tbsp. BBQ sauce and sprinkle with 1 tbsp. sugar.

7. Grill for 4 minutes, turn, baste and sprinkle again, then grill for another 4 minutes or until bubbling. ENJOY!

# THAI CHICKEN MEATLOAF
## SERVES 4

*"Thai?"* Did someone say *"Thai"?*

---

## INGREDIENTS

- 500g chicken (or turkey) mince
- 1 cup freshly grated breadcrumbs
  (I used 4 slices wholemeal bread)
- 1 red capsicum, diced
- 3 bunches of baby pak choy

## + GOURMET GARDEN

- 2 to 3 tbsp. Gourmet Garden Thai Stir-In Seasoning
- 1 tbsp. Gourmet Garden Lemongrass Stir-In Paste

## METHOD

1. In a large bowl, combine the chicken, breadcrumbs, capsicum, Thai Seasoning and lemongrass.

2. Season with sea salt and cracked pepper and stir well to combine.

3. Line a loaf tin with baking paper.

4. Trim the ends from the pak choy.

5. Into the loaf tin, spread half the chicken mixture.

6. Layer across all of the pak choy.

7. Top with remaining chicken mixture.

8. Place the tin in the slow cooker.

9. Cover and cook on LOW for 6 to 7 hours or HIGH for 3 to 4 hours.

10. Remove and rest for 10 minutes before slicing to serve with your favourite Asian Salad.

# SERVES 6

This is a super easy dinner to make and knowing that a chicken leg with the skin removed after cooking is only 180 calories makes me happy that I can have my chicken and eat it too! *NOTE:* A chicken leg with skin intact is 260 calories.

## INGREDIENTS

- 12 drumsticks, remove excess skin
- 420g can condensed tomato soup
- 35g packet French onion soup

## + GOURMET GARDEN

- 2 tbsp. Gourmet Garden Chive Stir-In Paste

## METHOD

1. Place the drumsticks in a slow cooker and season with cracked pepper.
2. In a jug, stir together the tomato soup, French onion soup and ½ cup water.
3. Pour over the drumsticks.
4. Toss to coat well.
6. Cover and cook on LOW for 4 to 5 hours or until the chicken is tender.
6. With 10 minutes to go, stir in chives and season to taste.

OPTIONAL: Serve with mashed potatoes, steamed beans and sautéed zucchini.

& CHIVES

LA

# MB

The benefits of using a slow cooker are endless. Not only does it add ease and convenience to a busy kitchen, but it helps create a beautifully tender, fragrant and hearty one pot meal every time, without fail.

# APRICOT BRAISED LAMB CHOPS

## SERVES 4

### INGREDIENTS

- 1kg lamb forequarter chops, trimmed
- 2 cups dried apricots, cut in half
- 3 tbsp. Dijon mustard
- 1 cup red wine

### + GOURMET GARDEN

- 1 tbsp. Gourmet Garden Garlic Stir-In Paste

### METHOD

1. Place the lamb chops in the slow cooker.

2. In a medium mixing bowl, combine apricots, mustard and garlic.

3. Spread this mixture over the lamb, then pour in the red wine.

4. Season with sea salt and cracked pepper.

5. Cook on LOW for 6 to 8 hours or HIGH for 3 to 4 hours.

6. The tender meat will literally melt in your mouth and is so enjoyable served with the plump, juicy apricots and jus that results.

# CLASSIC LAMB SHANKS *in a Garlic Red Wine Jus*

## SERVES 4

Lamb shanks and slow cooking are a match made in heaven, the meat simply slides from the bones and melts in your mouth.

---

### INGREDIENTS

- ½ cup plain flour
- 4 French-trimmed lamb shanks
- 200g bottle caramelised onions
- ¾ cup red wine

### + GOURMET GARDEN

- 2 tbsp. Gourmet Garden Garlic Stir-In Paste
- 1 tbsp. Gourmet Garden Rosemary Stir-In Paste

### METHOD

1. Season the flour with sea salt and cracked pepper, and mix well.

2. Coat the lamb shanks in the seasoned flour, then place in the slow cooker.

3. Pour over the caramelised onions and season.

4. In a separate bowl, mix red wine, garlic and rosemary.

5. Pour over the shanks.

6. Cover and cook on LOW for 6 to 8 hours or until the lamb is soft and falling off the bones.

7. Remove the shanks to plates and serve with the delicious gravy that results.

# LAMB, LENTIL & LEMONGRASS CURRY

## SERVES 4

### INGREDIENTS

- 1kg lamb (boneless shoulder or chump), diced
- ½ cup red lentils
- 2 tbsp. yellow curry paste
- 410g can crushed tomatoes with herbs

### + GOURMET GARDEN

- 2 tbsp. Gourmet Garden Lemongrass Stir-In Paste

### METHOD

1. Place the lamb in the slow cooker and sprinkle over the lentils.

2. In a bowl, mix together curry paste, tomatoes, lemongrass and ½ cup of water.

3. Add to the lamb and stir to combine.

4. Cover and cook on LOW for 6 to 8 hours or until the meat is deliciously tender.

5. To serve, season with a little more lemongrass and cracked pepper.

# ROSEMARY & GARLIC LEG OF LAMB

## SERVES 4

---

## INGREDIENTS

- 2 lemons, juice and zest
- ½ cup honey
- 2kg leg of lamb (bone-in)

## + GOURMET GARDEN

- 1 tbsp. Gourmet Garden Garlic Stir-In Paste
- 2 tbsp. Gourmet Garden Rosemary Stir-In Paste

## METHOD

1. In a small bowl, mix together lemon juice and zest, honey, garlic and rosemary.

2. Season the lamb with sea salt and cracked pepper and place in the slow cooker.

3. Pour over the lemon and honey mixture.

4. Cook on LOW for 8 hours.

5. With 2 hours to go, turn the roast over, baste, cover and continue to cook.

6. Serve sliced, drizzled with the yummy jus that remains.

**OPTIONAL:** Serve with creamy polenta, sautéed asparagus and steamed broccoli.

FRENCH
CASSE

# SERVES 4

## INGREDIENTS

- 1kg lamb forequarter chops, trimmed
- 35g packet French onion soup
- 410g can crushed tomatoes
- 8 baby carrots, trimmed

## + GOURMET GARDEN

- 2 tbsp. Gourmet Garden Lightly Dried Mixed Herbs

## METHOD

1. Place all the ingredients in the slow cooker.
2. Season with cracked pepper and stir to combine.
3. Cook on LOW for 6 to 8 hours or on HIGH for 3 to 4 hours until the meat is fork tender and melting off the bone.

I LAMB
ROLE

SIMPLE
LAMB S
CASSE

# SERVES 4

This is such a warm, hearty dish. Doing the prep work in the morning and letting it simmer in the slow cooker all day means the house is filled with a delicious aroma the minute you return from a busy day, which is precisely the reason we ALL love slow cooking.

## INGREDIENTS

- 4 lamb shanks (1.2kg), trimmed
- 2 onions, peeled and chopped
- 35g French onion soup
- 2 tbsp. Worcestershire sauce

## + GOURMET GARDEN

- 1 tbsp. Gourmet Garden Garlic Stir-In Paste

## METHOD

1. Place the lamb shanks in a slow cooker.

2. Brush with garlic and season with cracked pepper.

3. Add the onions.

4. Into 1 cup of water, add the French onion soup and Worcestershire sauce and mix well.

5. Pour over the shanks.

6. Cover and cook on LOW for 6 to 8 hours until the lovely lamb is falling from the bones.

**OPTIONAL:** Serve with steamed green beans and creamy mashed potato.

HANK
ROLE

# SPRING LAMB
## SERVES 4

## INGREDIENTS

- 1kg lamb forequarter chops, trimmed
- ⅓ cup beef stock
- 12 cherry tomatoes
- 100g feta, cut into 1cm cubes

## + GOURMET GARDEN

- 1 tsp. Gourmet Garden Lightly Dried Chilli
- 2 tbsp. Gourmet Garden Mediterranean Stir-In Seasoning

## METHOD

1. Place the lamb in the slow cooker and season with sea salt and pepper.

2. Combine chilli and Mediterranean Seasoning with stock; pour over the lamb.

3. Scatter with cherry tomatoes and feta.

4. Cover and cook on LOW for 6 to 8 hours or HIGH for 3 to 4 hours.

5. Remove the lamb from slow cooker and serve drizzled with the tangy tomato, feta and juices that remain.

**OPTIONAL:** This is lovely served drizzled with the yummy jus that remains, and with steamed baby potatoes and greens.

# SPICY SAVOURY MINCE
## SERVES 4

## INGREDIENTS

- 1kg lamb mince
- 1 large brown onion, peeled and chopped
- 400g cauliflower cut into florets
- 3 tbsp. tomato paste

### + GOURMET GARDEN

- 3 tbsp. Gourmet Garden Moroccan Stir-In Seasoning
- 1 tbsp. Gourmet Garden Lemongrass Stir-In Paste

## METHOD

1. Place the mince, onion and cauliflower in the slow cooker.
2. Combine remaining ingredients (except lemongrass) with ½ cup water.
3. Pour over mince and mix well.
4. Cover and cook on LOW for 6 to 8 hours.
5. In the final 10 minutes, stir in the lemongrass and season to taste.

**OPTIONAL:** Serve with couscous, natural yoghurt and papadums.

# ORK

Pork is considered the world's most popular meat and if you are seeking a lean meat, pork is what you want. The fresh shoulder and upper part of the shoulder, the ham hocks, blade roasts and spare ribs are the very best cuts for the slow cooker.

ASIAN PORK

# SERVES 8

## INGREDIENTS

- ⅓ cup ketjap manis (sweet soy sauce)
- 2 tbsp. Chinese five-spice powder
- 2kg pork shoulder, remove the outer layer of fat and discard
- 2 cups shredded Chinese cabbage

## + GOURMET GARDEN

- 1 tbsp. Gourmet Garden Lightly Dried Ginger
- 1 tsp. Gourmet Garden Lightly Dried Chilli
- 1 tsp. Gourmet Garden Garlic Stir-In Paste

## METHOD

1. Place the ketjap manis, five-spice, ginger, chilli and garlic into the slow cooker and mix well.

2. Place the pork in the slow cooker and roll in the sauce to coat.

3. Cover and cook on LOW for 8 hours.

4. Using two forks, shred the meat completely.

5. Fold in the thinly sliced cabbage, distributing the sauce.

6. Sit this divine combination for 10 minutes before serving.

**OPTIONAL:** Serve on fresh, crispy sesame seed buns piled high with Asian Slaw.

# SERVES 4

## INGREDIENTS

- 2 x 420g can cannellini beans, drained
- 1kg smoked ham hocks
- 420g can 'Big Red' tomato soup
- ¼ cup pure maple syrup

## + GOURMET GARDEN

- 1 to 2 tbsp. Gourmet Garden Rosemary Stir-In Paste

## METHOD

1. Place all the ingredients in a slow cooker and season with sea salt and cracked pepper.

2. Note, the hocks have a thick skin, this is near impossible to remove until after being slow cooked.

3. Into the empty can of soup, add ½ cup water, swirl to remove all the soup and pour into the cooker and stir to combine.

4. Cover and cook on LOW for 6 to 8 hours.

5. Remove the hocks, peel back the skin (discard skin and bones), shred the ham from the bones and return the meat to the slow cooker.

6. Stir through before serving.

**OPTIONAL:** For a complete comfort meal, serve with toasted sourdough and or poached, fried or scrambled eggs and a sprinkle of Gourmet Garden Lightly Dried Basil.

BEANS

# BROWN SUGAR GLAZED CHOPS

## SERVES 6

---

## INGREDIENTS

- ¾ cup dried prunes
- ¼ cup brown sugar
- 2 tbsp. apple cider vinegar
- 6 pork forequarter chops, trimmed

## + GOURMET GARDEN

- 1 tbsp. Gourmet Garden Thyme Stir-In Paste

## METHOD

1. In a small mixing bowl combine the prunes, brown sugar, vinegar and thyme.

2. Place chops in the slow cooker and rub well with this paste.

3. Add ¼ cup water and season with sea salt and cracked pepper.

4. Cover and cook on LOW for 4 to 6 hours.

5. Serve each chop with a couple of prunes and drizzled with the rich flavourful sauce that results; it is quite runny so serve with rice to soak it up.

# EASIEST EVER SAUSAGE CASSEROLE

## SERVES 4

## INGREDIENTS

- ¼ cup BBQ sauce
- 410g can diced tomatoes
- 420g can cannellini beans, drained
- 8 pork sausages

## + GOURMET GARDEN

- 2 tbsp. Gourmet Garden Mediterranean Stir-In Seasoning
- 1 tbsp. Gourmet Garden Lightly Dried Parsley

## METHOD

1. Combine the BBQ sauce, tomatoes, beans and Mediterranean Seasoning in the slow cooker.

2. Swirl ½ cup water around the empty can of tomatoes to remove all the sauce, add.

3. Nestle the sausages into the sauce and turn to coat.

4. Cook on LOW for 4 hours or until done.

5. Sometimes (if I'm making this for my little 4-year old nephew) I will remove the sausages and slice, returning them to the slow cooker; either way it's yummy.

6. 10 minutes before serving, stir in the parsley.

**OPTIONAL:** Serve with rice or mashed potato, steamed greens and a sprinkle of parsley.

# PULLED PORK

I cannot urge you enough to start pulling pork. The pork shoulder is one of my secret weapons in the kitchen but to cook it into heavenly succulence requires time. The shoulder is a hard-working muscle and the meat is pretty tough but on a low, steady temperature, however, the gelatin in that tough shoulder melts and bastes the meat as it cooks... You cannot rush tenderness!

Place the meat in your slow cooker, pour in just enough liquid (beer, stock, vinegar) so the meat is partially submerged, then cover and cook slowly for 8 hours. This is entirely hands-off time. The pork is done when it literally flakes, falling effortlessly off the bone.

# FRUITY PULLED PORK WITH THYME
## SERVES 6

This is a sensational dish. The first time I tried it I felt like I was eating Christmas on a plate; rich, flavourful and ever so easy to prepare.

## INGREDIENTS

- 1.5kg boneless pork shoulder, remove the outer layer of fat
- 375g packet mixed dried fruit
- 1 cup BBQ sauce

### + GOURMET GARDEN

- 2 tbsp. Gourmet Garden Thyme Stir-In Paste

## METHOD

1. Place the pork into the slow cooker.

2. Baste with thyme and season with cracked pepper.

3. Add the dried fruit.

4. Pour BBQ sauce over all.

5. Cover and cook on LOW for 8 hours.

6. Using two forks, shred the pork, stirring to blend with the deliciously 'fruity' sauce.

7. Sit for 10 minutes before serving.

**OPTIONAL:** Serve with crusty baguette and a fresh garden salad.

PULLED
BURGE

# MAKES 12 *FABULOUS* BURGERS

I have made this dish over a dozen times; my boys and all their friends just LOVE it... I love it too because it's easy. I serve it on fresh, crunchy bread rolls for my boys, and on a crisp lettuce leaf for the adults. Topped with coleslaw, these pork burgers are a HUGE HIT with everyone!

## INGREDIENTS

- 1.5kg boneless pork shoulder, remove the outer layer of fat
- ⅔ cup apple cider vinegar
- 1 - 1½ cups smoky BBQ sauce

## + GOURMET GARDEN

- 1 tbsp. Gourmet Garden Garlic Stir-In Paste

## METHOD

1. Trim the excess fat from the pork roast.

2. Rub with garlic.

3. Place in the slow cooker and add the vinegar.

4. Cover and cook on LOW for 8 hours.

5. Drain the liquid, and using two forks, shred the meat, pulling it apart (it reminds me of fairy-floss that's how easily it shreds).

6. Stir the smoky BBQ sauce through the meat, I highly recommend a Vintage Smokehouse BBQ Sauce for the best flavour.

PORK
RS

# THYME & APRICOT GLAZED PORK CHOPS

## SERVES 6

### INGREDIENTS

- 6 pork forequarter chops
- 200g dried apricots
- 1 large red capsicum, sliced into wedges
- 1 cup BBQ sauce

### + GOURMET GARDEN

- 2 tbsp. Gourmet Garden Thyme Stir-In Paste

### METHOD

1. Trim all excess fat from the pork chops, then nestle into the slow cooker.
2. Brush with thyme.
3. Add dried apricots and capsicum.
4. Pour the BBQ sauce over all.
5. Cover and cook on LOW for 4 to 6 hours.
6. Transfer the chops to a serving platter, and spoon over the yummy sauce.

# TEXAN PORK CHOPS
## SERVES 6

### INGREDIENTS

- 6 pork forequarter chops, trimmed
- 300g jar salsa
- 2 tbsp. chopped jalapeños

### + GOURMET GARDEN

- 1 tbsp. Gourmet Garden Lightly Dried Coriander

### METHOD

1. Place the pork chops into the slow cooker and season with sea salt and cracked pepper.

2. Pour over the salsa and jalapeños.

3. Into the empty salsa jar, add ¼ cup water, gently swirl and add to the mix.

4. Cover and cook on LOW for 4 to 6 hours.

5. In the last 10 minutes stir in the coriander.

OPTIONAL: Assemble any way you want. But I tend to serve the tender chops on a small bed of rice, drizzled with the tasty sauce and sprinkled with a little extra coriander.

# JPS

No longer do I feel anxious or exhausted when asked, "What's for dinner Mum?" Whether a soup, stew or casserole, prepare the slow cooker in the morning, turn it on and you'll feel instant relief returning home after a busy day. All you have to do is walk in and plate up! Eat earlier. Relax easier. Go to bed sooner.

# CURRIED CARROT SOUP

## SERVES 4

Here's a soup that is healthy, tastes good and makes me feel warm. A nutrient packed soup providing my whole family refuge from those chilly winter nights.

---

## INGREDIENTS

- 1½ tsp. curry powder, or to taste
- 1 large leek, white part only, sliced
- 4 large carrots, chopped
- 1 sweet potato, peeled and chopped

## + GOURMET GARDEN

- 1 tbsp. Gourmet Garden Garlic Stir-In Paste
- 1 tbsp. Gourmet Garden Lightly Dried Basil

## METHOD

1. Place all ingredients in a slow cooker (except the basil).

2. Add 1.5 litres of water and stir to combine.

3. Cover and cook on LOW for 4 to 6 hours.

4. Cool for 10 minutes.

5. Puree until smooth.

6. Stir through basil and season to taste.

# GINGER, LEMONGRASS & PUMPKIN SOUP

## SERVES 4

There's something about the flavour combinations in this soup. I love the bold taste of ginger mixed with the fresh, citrus flavour of lemongrass.

## INGREDIENTS

- 1kg pumpkin, peeled and cut into chunks
- 1 large brown onion, peeled and chopped
- 1 litre chicken stock
- 4 tbsp. sour cream

## + GOURMET GARDEN

- 1 tbsp. Gourmet Garden Ginger Stir-In Paste
- 1 tbsp. Gourmet Garden Lemongrass Stir-In Paste

## METHOD

1. Place all the ingredients (except sour cream) into the slow cooker.

2. Cover and cook on LOW for 4 hours or HIGH for 2 hours.

3. Cool for 10 minutes.

4. Using a stick blender, blend until smooth.

5. Season to taste and serve with a dollop of sour cream.

# SERVES 4

This soup is definite comfort food. On a cold evening, I'm convinced it is the most delicious way to warm up.

## INGREDIENTS

- 4 tbsp. butter, melted
- 6 brown onions, peeled and thinly sliced
- 1.5 litres beef stock

## + GOURMET GARDEN

- 2 tbsp. Gourmet Garden Thyme Stir-In Paste

## METHOD

1. Pour the butter into the slow cooker.

2. Add the onions and stir to coat well, season and cook on HIGH for 20 minutes.

3. Meanwhile mix together the beef stock and thyme.

4. Pour over the buttery onions, cover and cook on LOW for 6 hours, honestly, the longer you leave this soup the lovelier it is.

SOUP

# LENTIL & TOMATO SOUP
## SERVES 4

Take off winter's chill with a bowl of nourishing, steaming soup.

## INGREDIENTS

- 1 large celery stalk, chopped
- 1 onion, peeled and chopped
- 420g can condensed tomato soup
- 420g can brown lentils, drained and rinsed

## + GOURMET GARDEN

- 2 tbsp. Gourmet Garden Lightly Dried Parsley

## METHOD

1. Place all ingredients (except parsley) in the slow cooker.

2. Then fill the empty tomato soup can with water, gently swirl and add to the mix.

3. Season with cracked pepper.

4. Cook on LOW for 6 hours.

5. Cool for 10 minutes.

6. Puree until smooth.

7. Stir through parsley and season to taste.

# PEA & HAM SOUP

## SERVES 4

This soup is soul-food; simply pop everything in the slow cooker, come back six hours later and you have a classic soup with flavours to satisfy everyone.

## INGREDIENTS

- 2 brown onions, peeled and roughly chopped
- 1.2kg ham hocks
- 500g green peas
- 1 litre chicken stock

## + GOURMET GARDEN

- 1 tsp. Gourmet Garden Garlic Stir-In Paste
- 1 tsp. Gourmet Garden Dill Stir-In Paste

## METHOD

1. Place all the ingredients (except dill) in the slow cooker.

2. Season with cracked pepper.

3. Cover and cook on LOW for 6 hours.

4. Remove the cover, and cool for 10 minutes.

5. Strip the meat from the hocks, discarding the bones and skin.

6. Return the meat to the soup, add dill.

7. Using a stick blender, blend until smooth.

POTATO
LEEKS

# SERVES 4

This wonderfully rich, creamy soup with a velvety texture is pure comfort food.

## INGREDIENTS

- 4 potatoes, peeled and chopped
- 2 leeks, white part only, chopped
- 1 litre vegetable stock
- ½ cup sour cream

## + GOURMET GARDEN

- 1 tsp. Gourmet Garden Garlic Stir-In Paste

## METHOD

1. Place the potatoes, leeks and garlic into the slow cooker.
2. Season with sea salt and pepper.
3. Pour over the stock plus 1 cup water and stir.
4. Cook on LOW for 4 to 6 hours.
5. Cool for 10 minutes.
6. Using a stick blender, blend until smooth.
7. Add the sour cream and stir to combine.

**OPTIONAL:** Finely slice some of the rimmed leek greens. Shallow-fry in hot oil until golden, drain and use as garnish on this delicious soup.

# SPRING VEGETABLE SOUP
## SERVES 4

A scrummy soup loaded with veggies that is my go-to bowl of nourishment.

## INGREDIENTS

- 2 leeks, white part only, chopped
- 2 large celery stalks, chopped
- 3 zucchinis, chopped
- 1 litre chicken stock

## + GOURMET GARDEN

- 1 tbsp. Gourmet Garden Mint Stir-In Paste

## METHOD

1. Place all the ingredients (except mint) plus ½ cup water in the slow cooker.

2. Cover and cook on LOW for 4 hours or HIGH for 2 hours.

3. Cool for 10 minutes.

4. Add the mint and using a stick blender, blend until smooth.

5. Season to taste before ladling among serving bowls.

# THAI CHICKEN & CORN SOUP
## SERVES 8

Thai cuisine is known for its delicate balance and emphasis on the five fundamental taste senses; sweet, sour, salty, bitter and spicy. Gourmet Garden's Thai Seasoning encompasses all in the perfect blend of finely chopped lemongrass, ginger, coriander and chilli resulting in authentic flavoured Thai every time.

### INGREDIENTS

- 1.25 litres chicken stock
- 400g creamed corn (less if you prefer)
- 2 cups leftover chicken meat, shredded
- 2 shallots, sliced diagonally

### + GOURMET GARDEN

- 2 tbsp. Gourmet Garden Thai Stir-In Seasoning
- 1 tbsp. Gourmet Garden Lightly Dried Ginger

### METHOD

1. Pour the stock into the slow cooker.
2. Add the creamed corn and stir.
3. Add remaining ingredients and season.
4. Cook on LOW for 4 hours or HIGH for 2 hours.
5. Cool for 5 minutes before serving.

# SERVES 8

Look no further for a traditional favourite than this rich Tomato & Thyme Soup. Made with minimal ingredients and full of flavour it will be your easiest go-to soup this winter.

## INGREDIENTS

- 2 x 800g can diced tomatoes
- 1 litre vegetable stock
- 2 tbsp. brown sugar

## + GOURMET GARDEN

- 2 tbsp. Gourmet Garden Thyme Stir-In Paste
- 1 tbsp. Gourmet Garden Garlic Stir-In Paste

## METHOD

1. Place all the ingredients in the slow cooker; and season generously with sea salt and cracked pepper.

2. Cook on LOW for 4 hours or HIGH for 2 hours.

3. Cool for 10 minutes.

4. Using a stick blender, blend until smooth.

**OPTIONAL:** Serve with a slice of crusty bread.

VEGE

# ARIAN

When you think of slow cooker meals, vegetarian recipes are not often plentiful. Vegetables may not take that long to cook, but the addition of legumes and beans and the slow bubbling of a sauce enriches an entire meal, changing the flavour of your usual ingredients – and that is worth slow cooking.

# SERVES 8

This sauce is a definite set and forget. Toss all the ingredients into the slow cooker and walk away. There is no need to babysit the pot all day and the rich, full flavour that result is truly amazing.

## INGREDIENTS

- 200g butter, softened
- 2 x 800g cans whole tomatoes
- 4 brown onions, peeled and quartered

## + GOURMET GARDEN

- 1 tbsp. Gourmet Garden Lightly Dried Basil

## METHOD

1. Place the butter in the slow cooker on HIGH, cover until melted, 5 minutes.

2. Add the tomatoes and onions, season and stir.

3. Cover and cook on LOW for 6 to 8 hours
   (to be honest, the longer you leave this the richer the flavours become).

4. 10 minutes before serving, stir through the basil.

OPTIONAL: Serve over your favourite pasta, sprinkled with Parmesan cheese.

# LENTIL TACOS
## SERVES 4

### INGREDIENTS

- 2 cups dried brown lentils, rinsed
- 1 brown onion, peeled and sliced
- 2 cups vegetable stock
- 35g packet Reduced Salt Taco seasoning

### + GOURMET GARDEN

- 2 tbsp. Gourmet Garden Lightly Dried Coriander

### METHOD

1. Place all ingredients (except the coriander) in a slow cooker.

2. Stir to combine.

3. Cook on LOW for 4 to 6 hours, or until the lentils are tender. Stir in a little extra liquid if needed.

4. Stir in half the coriander, serve sprinkled with the remaining.

**OPTIONAL:** Serve piled high into soft toasty tacos along with your favourite fillings.

# MEDITERRANEAN MUSHROOM RISOTTO

## SERVES 4

## INGREDIENTS

- 2 tbsp. butter, melted
- 1 cup Arborio rice
- 1 litre vegetable stock
- 500g button mushrooms, cut in half

## + GOURMET GARDEN

- 1½ tsp. Gourmet Garden Mediterranean Stir-In Seasoning
- 1 tsp. Gourmet Garden Garlic Stir-In Paste
- 1 tbsp. Gourmet Garden Lightly Dried Parsley

## METHOD

1. Turn the slow cooker on HIGH.
2. Add the butter, Mediterranean Seasoning and garlic.
3. Season and stir to combine.
4. After 10 minutes add the rice and stir to coat.
5. Pour in the stock plus 1 cup of water and stir again.
6. Cover and cook on HIGH for 1½ hours.
7. Stir through the mushrooms.
8. Cook for a further 30 to 45 minutes or until the rice is tender.
9. Remove the lid and stir in parsley.
10. Season to taste.

**OPTIONAL:** Serve sprinkled with Parmesan cheese and a little more parsley and remember never wash the rice. The starch is essential for keeping the risotto rice nice and creamy.

# MOROCCAN CHICKPEA STEW

## SERVES 4

Capture the exotic flavours of Morocco with Gourmet Garden Moroccan Stir-In Seasoning. A perfect blend of coriander, ginger, garlic and cumin, it will add life to kebabs, tagines, couscous and this delicious stew.

## INGREDIENTS

- 420g can chickpeas, drained
- 1 small head of cauliflower (250g), cut into florets
- 410g diced tomatoes with garlic
- 3 cups vegetable stock

## + GOURMET GARDEN

- 2 tbsp. Gourmet Garden Moroccan Stir-In Seasoning
- 1 tbsp. Gourmet Garden Lightly Dried Coriander

## METHOD

1. Place all the ingredients (except coriander) in a slow cooker and season with sea salt and cracked pepper.
2. Cook on LOW for 4 hours.
3. With 10 minutes remaining, stir through the coriander.

**OPTIONAL:** Add a cup of chopped, mixed vegetables in the last hour. Serve with couscous and a dollop of natural yoghurt.

# VEGETABLE FRITTATA

## SERVES 6

---

## INGREDIENTS

- 1 (packed) cup baby spinach
- 8 eggs
- 1 cup grated Mozzarella cheese
- 8 cherry tomatoes, halved

## + GOURMET GARDEN

- 2 tbsp. Gourmet Garden Chives Stir-In Paste

## METHOD

1. Line the slow cooker with baking paper.

2. Cover the base with spinach.

3. In a large bowl whisk together eggs and chives.

4. Season generously with sea salt and cracked pepper.

5. Add ¾ cup of Mozzarella and whisk to combine.

6. Pour this mixture over the spinach.

7. Sprinkle with remaining Mozzarella.

8. Add the cherry tomato halves.

9. Cook on HIGH for 1 to 2 hours, or until set when a knife inserted in the centre removes clean.

ZUCCH
SLICE

# SERVES 6

## INGREDIENTS

- 9 eggs
- 1 cup self raising flour
- 2 zucchinis, grated and squeezed gently to remove excess liquid
- 1 cup grated cheddar cheese

## + GOURMET GARDEN

- 1 tbsp. Gourmet Garden Chives Stir-In Paste
- 1 tbsp. Gourmet Garden Lightly Dried Chilli

## METHOD

1. Line the base of the slow cooker bowl with baking paper.
2. Beat the eggs in a large bowl, add the flour and beat again until smooth.
3. Add the zucchini, cheese, chives and chilli.
4. Season generously with sea salt and cracked pepper then stir to combine.
5. Pour into the prepared slow cooker.
6. Cook on HIGH for 1 to 2 hours, or until set when a knife inserted in the centre removes clean.

**OPTIONAL:** Serve, sliced with a fresh, garden salad for lunch or dinner.

# HERB PAIRING GUIDE

*For more on herbs visit gourmetgarden.com*

The secret to any meal is FLAVOUR and one of the easiest and healthiest ways to add flavour is with herbs and spices; which were not meant to live alone! There are so many ingredients you can pair them with to create amazing, flavourful meals. I hope this *Herb Pairing Guide* will help you add the magic of herbs into your everyday cooking.

## BASIL
Anise
Capsicum
Chicken
Chilli
Clove
Coconut
Egg
Garlic
Goat's Cheese
Lemon
Lime
Mint
Olive Oil
Onion
Oregano
Parmesan Cheese
Pasta
Pinenuts
Raspberry
Shellfish
Spinach
Thyme
Tomato
Walnut
Zucchini

## CHILLI (Mild, Hot)
Almond
Anchovy
Anise
Avocado
Bacon
Basil
Beef
Broccoli
Butternut Squash
Cabbage
Capsicum
Cauliflower
Chicken
Chocolate
Coconut
Coriander
Egg
Eggplant (Aubergine)
Garlic
Ginger
Goat's Cheese
Hard Cheese
Lemon
Lemongrass
Lime
Liver
Mango
Mint

Noodles
Oily Fish
Olive
Orange
Oregano
Oyster
Parsley
Peanut
Pineapple
Pork
Potato
Rosemary
Shallots
Shellfish
Thyme
Tomato
Walnut
Watermelon

## CHIVES
Cheese
Chilli
Egg
Garlic
Ginger
Lemon
Mushrooms
Parsley
Potato

Sesame oil
Sour Cream
Soy sauce
Tarragon
Veal
Vinegar

## CORIANDER
Avocado
Carrot
Chicken
Chilli
Coconut
Coriander Seed
Cumin
Fish Sauce
Garlic
Goat's Cheese
Lamb
Lemon
Lemongrass
Lime
Mango
Mint
Orange
Parsley
Peanut
Pineapple
Pork

Potato
Shellfish
Soy Sauce
Tomato
Watermelon
White Fish

## DILL
Avocado
Asparagus
Beef
Beetroot
Carrot
Coconut
Cucumber
Egg
Fish
Lamb
Lemon
Mayonnaise
Mint
Mushrooms
Pea
Pork
Potato
Salmon
Shellfish
Smoked fish
White fish  Almond

## GARLIC

Anchovy
Basil
Beans
Beef
Broccoli
Cabbage
Cauliflower
Chicken
Chilli
Coriander
Cucumber
Eggplant
Ginger
Goat's cheese
Hazelnut
Lamb
Liver
Mint
Mushroom
Noodles
Oily fish
Olives
Onions
Parsley
Pasta
Pork
Potato
Rosemary
Shellfish
Soft Cheese
Spinach
Thyme
Tomato
Truffle
Turmeric
Walnut

## GINGER

Almond
Apricot
Beef
Butternut Squash
Cabbage
Cardamom
Carrot
Chilli
Chocolate

Cinnamon
Clove
Coffee
Coriander
Egg
Eggplant
Garlic
Honey
Lemon
Lemongrass
Lime
Mango
Melon
Mint
Oily Fish
Onion
Orange
Pork
Rhubarb
Sugar
Tea
Tomato
Vanilla
White Fish

## LEMONGRASS

Basil
Berries
Chicken
Chilli
Citrus
Coconut
Coriander
Corn
Fish
Galangal
Garlic
Ginger
Lamb
Lime
Noodles
Palm Sugar
Pork
Prawns
Rice
Scallops
Shallots
Soy
Tropical Fruits

Turmeric
Vanilla

## MINT

Anise
Asparagus
Avocado
Basil
Beef
Blackcurrant
Black Pudding
Chilli
Chocolate
Cinnamon
Coriander
Cucumber
Cumin
Dill
Fig
Garlic
Ginger
Globe Artichoke
Goats Cheese
Lamb
Lemon
Lime
Mango
Melon
Mushroom
Oily Fish
Onion
Orange
Parsley
Pea
Peanut
Potato
Raspberry
Strawberry
Watermelon
Yoghurt

## OREGANO

Basil
Beef
Bread
Capsicum
Chicken
Chilli
Eggplant

Feta cheese
Fish
Garlic
Olive
Parsley
Pasta
Rosemary
Spinach
Thyme
Tomato
Zucchini

## PARSLEY

Bacon
Basil
Beef
Butter
Caper
Carrot
Chicken
Chilli
Chives
Coriander
Dill
Egg
Fish
Garlic
Lemon
Mint
Mushroom
Oily Fish
Oregano
Oyster
Pasta
Pepper
Pork
Potato
Pizza
Rosemary
Shellfish
Smoked Fish
Thyme
Tomato
Walnut
White Fish

## ROSEMARY

Almond
Anchovy

Apricot
Bread
Butternut Squash
Chestnut
Chicken
Chocolate
Garlic
Goat's Cheese
Grape
Hazelnut
Lamb
Lemon
Mushroom
Oily Fish
Olive
Onion
Orange
Parmesan cheese
Pea
Pork
Potato
Rhubarb
Tomato
Watermelon

## THYME

Bacon
Beef
Chicken
Chocolate
Cinnamon
Garlic
Goat's Cheese
Lamb
Lemon
Mushroom
Oily Fish
Olive
Onion
Orange
Pork
Potato
Shellfish
Tomato
White Fish
Wine

# BIBLIOGRAPHY

## WEBSITES

**Recipes and Product Range**
http://www.gourmetgarden.com/en/recipe

**Top 50 Slow Cooker Recipes**
http://www.taste.com.au/gallery/
top+50+slow+cooker+recipes,211

**Slow Cooker Recipes**
http://www.bestrecipes.com.au/collections/slow-
cooker-recipes

## BOOKS & MAGAZINES

McCosker, Kim. **4 Ingredients.**
4 Ingredients. PTY LTD. PO BOX 400 Caloundra QLD,
Australia. 2012. Adapted recipes from.

McCosker, Kim. **4 Ingredients One Pot One Bowl.**
4 Ingredients. PTY LTD. PO BOX 400 Caloundra QLD,
Australia. 2012. Adapted recipes from.

McCosker, Kim. **4 Ingredients Menu Planning.**
4 Ingredients. PTY LTD. PO BOX 400 Caloundra QLD,
Australia. 2013. Adapted recipes from.

Segnit, Niki. **The Flavour Thesaurus.**
Bloomsbury Publishing Plc. 50 Bedford Square,
London WC1B 3DP. 2010. Provided inspiration for
Herb Pairing Guide.

O'Dea, Stephanie. **5 Ingredients or Less Slow
Cooker Cookbook.**
Houghton Mifflin Harcourt Publishing Company.
215 Park Avenue South. New York, New York, 10003.
2015. Provided inspiration for layout and recipes.

Christie, Pauline. **Slow Cooker Central.**
Harper Collins Publishers. Level 13, 210 Elizabeth
Street, Sydney 2000, Australia. 2015. Provided
inspiration for Reasons to Love Your Slow Cooker –
and – Sensational Slow Cooker Tips.